I0518427

# GOD'S
# GOT
# YOU

## YOU GOT THIS

**Five Minutes A Day To Strengthen Your Faith**
By: D. Nichole French

All Rights Reserved.
No part of this book may be used or reproduced by any means, graphic, electronic, or mechanical, including photocopying, or by any information storage retrieval system without the written permission of the owner except in the case of brief quotations in articles and reviews.
Copyright © 2024 by D. Nichole French
ISBN: 979-8-9907017-1-7

# FORWARD

This book is an invitation to navigate the tempests of life—be they illness, loss, uncertainty, or personal trials—with courage and an unwavering spirit. In these pages, you embark on the path of becoming a "MasterPeace," mastering not only the external challenges life throws your way but also the internal turmoil they create.

"MasterPeaces" are created through the storm. They are the product of our struggles, crafted from our battles with fear, stress, and the quest for peace amidst chaos. This devotional offers daily reflections, scriptures, and prayers as tools to help you paint your life's canvas with resilience, hope, and faith.

As you journey through each page, remember that every challenge is an opportunity to grow stronger, more peaceful, and more connected to your faith. You are not merely surviving; you are crafting a masterpiece of your existence, a testament to the beauty that arises from adversity.

May you find solace, strength, and transformation in these words, and may your spirit become unshakable as you create your unique "MasterPeace." God's Got You and You Got This.

With Love from one MasterPeace to another,

**D Nichole**

GOD'S GOT YOU YOU GOT THIS

# TABLE OF CONTENTS

# INTRODUCTION

Welcome to this 30-day journey of reflection, healing, and growth. Whether you are facing the challenges of life firsthand or walking alongside someone who is, this devotional is designed to be a source of comfort, strength, and inspiration. In the coming days, you will be invited to explore deep questions of faith, resilience, and the power of a hopeful spirit.

This book is more than just a collection of daily readings; it is a journey we will embark on together. Each day's content is crafted to speak to the heart, offering a moment of peace and reflection in the midst of life's storms. The scriptures, prayers, and reflections are chosen to resonate with the unique challenges and fears that come with life as it lifes.

As you engage with each day's material, you are encouraged to reflect deeply, pray earnestly, and embrace the affirmations fully. The journal prompts and interactive challenges are there to guide you in applying these insights to your life, fostering a sense of personal growth and spiritual depth.

This journey is about finding strength in places you might not have looked before—within your vulnerabilities, in the quiet moments of peace, and in the hopeful gaze toward the future. It is about recognizing that even in the midst of challenges, there is a profound beauty and strength in the human spirit, a resilience that can be harnessed, and a joy that can be cultivated.

As you turn these pages, may you find solace in the words, strength in the prayers, and inspiration in the reflections. May this devotional serve as a beacon of hope, guiding you toward a path of healing and peace. Welcome to your 30-day journey—may it be a transformative experience filled with moments of grace, understanding, and profound personal growth.

# CHAPTER 01  WEEK 1
## FINDING STRENGTH IN VULNERABILITY

# Day 1
# Embracing the Journey Ahead

**Scripture:** "I can do all things through Christ who strengthens me."
**Philippians 4:13 NIV**

August 24, 2021, is a day I will never forget, I was diagnosed with Stage 3 breast cancer. I found myself numb and overcome with fear, much like you feel now. As I sat there in that room, wondering how am I going to handle this, I was reminded of our innate human resilience. The same resilience that's within you, even if it feels out of reach right now.

I took a step forward on my journey, not knowing where it would lead but understanding that the journey itself was a step through hardship. With each treatment, I could sense God's subtle guidance, like a quiet conversation that eased my fears. It was a path of healing, a path that showed me that even in my lowest moments, I wasn't walking alone. As you face this tough chapter in your life, I want to share that sense of companionship with you.

The path ahead is uncertain but with each step, you move toward completion.

Your journey, like mine, is both deeply personal and divinely touched. Trust that the challenges are not just trials but opportunities for growth and that in your vulnerability, God's strength is ready to carry you through. Embrace the trek, my friend, for it's in the walking that we find our way back to hope, step by step.

**Prayer:** "Heavenly Father, as I embark on this journey, grant me the courage to embrace my vulnerabilities, knowing that in my weakness, your strength is revealed. Guide me to find peace in being open and authentic with myself and others. Amen."

**Affirmation:** "Each day, I am growing stronger and more resilient."

**Journal Prompt:** Reflect on what vulnerability means to you and a moment when acknowledging your vulnerabilities led you to strength or support.

_____
_____
_____
_____
_____
_____
_____
_____
_____
_____

**Challenge:** Share a personal fear or hope about this journey with someone you trust, opening a dialogue about vulnerability.

# Day 2
# The Power of Positive Thought

**Scripture:** "For as he thinks in his heart, so is he."
**Proverbs 23:7 NIV**

Our thoughts have a profound impact on our spirit and our journey through life's challenges. The Bible tells us the way we think in our heart defines who we are. I learned pretty quickly that the more I dwelled on the negative thoughts the more they festered. With my eyes wide open, running full speed I would just jump into the rabbit hole of fear with no ladder to climb out. I was torturing myself and was pretty good at it.

Today, we went into how a positive mindset, rooted in faith, can transform our experiences of vulnerability into opportunities for strength. The Bible teaches us the importance of renewing our minds, which allows us to see God's good and perfect will. By focusing on God's promises and maintaining a hopeful outlook, we can navigate our vulnerabilities with a sense of peace and purpose. Let's explore how cultivating positive thoughts can lead us to a deeper understanding and trust in God's plan.

**Prayer:** "Lord, infuse my spirit with positivity, especially in moments of doubt and fear. Help me to see Your light in every situation, transforming my thoughts into a source of strength. Amen."

**Affirmation:** "I choose to focus on the positive and see the beauty in each day."

**Journal Prompt:** Identify a situation where a positive outlook transformed a challenge into an opportunity for growth. How did this perspective change the outcome?

_____

_____

_____

_____

_____

_____

_____

_____

_____

_____

**Challenge:** Start your day by writing down three positive affirmations about yourself, focusing on your inner strengths and resilience.

# Day 3
# Accepting Support from Loved Ones

**Scripture:** "Two are better than one... For if they fall, one will lift up his companion." **Ecclesiastes 4:9-10 NIV**

When you are use to being independent it is hard to admit you need and even harder to ask for; HELP. Ask me how I know. One of God's greatest gifts to us is the community of family and friends He places in our lives. There is a strength that comes from accepting support, showing that vulnerability in reaching out is not a sign of weakness but a step towards healing and growth.

Just as Aaron and Hur held up Moses' arms, our loved ones offer us the strength we might not have on our own. Opening up to accept help is a powerful act of trust, both in our community and in God's provision through them. Let this day remind you that in every "ask" for help, there's an echo of God's love calling us to lean on each other.

**Prayer:** "Gracious God, thank You for the gift of community and the support of loved ones. Help me to open my heart to receive help with grace, knowing that we are all stronger together. Amen."

**Affirmation:** "I am grateful for the love and support that surrounds me."

**Journal Prompt:** Think of a time when accepting help was difficult for you. What emotions did you feel, and how did it ultimately benefit you?

_____

_____

_____

_____

_____

_____

_____

_____

_____

**Challenge:** Reach out to a friend or family member and express your appreciation for their support. If you're facing a challenge, let them know how they can help you.

# Day 4
# The Courage to Be Vulnerable

**Scripture:** "Be strong and courageous. Do not be afraid; do not be discouraged, for the Lord your God will be with you wherever you go." **Joshua 1:9 NIV**

I remember the first time I said I had been diagnosed with breast cancer out loud. I felt as if someone had thrown me out naked in the middle of 5 o'clock traffic. Vulnerable, weak, and exposed. "How will they see me now? I am no one's charity case. I don't need your pity", these are just a few of the thoughts that came racing to my mind.

Vulnerability often feels like standing at the edge of a cliff, with the choice to either step back into safety or trust the wind to carry us. Today is about finding the courage to choose trust—to be open about our fears, hopes, and the struggles that shape us. It's in these moments of openness that our relationship with God deepens, as we allow Him into our most guarded spaces.

This courage doesn't just change us; it invites others to be brave in their faith and vulnerabilities too. Let today be a testament to the strength that blooms from the courage to be truly seen, both by God and those we walk with.

**Prayer:** "Dear God, grant me the courage to expose my fears and uncertainties, trusting that vulnerability is not a weakness but a path to genuine connection and strength. Amen."

**Affirmation:** "In my vulnerability lies my strength and courage."

**Journal Prompt:** Write about a fear that holds you back from being fully vulnerable with others. What step can you take to address this fear?

_____

_____

_____

_____

_____

_____

_____

_____

_____

_____

**Challenge:** Share a personal struggle with a friend or in a support group, embracing the strength that comes from vulnerability.

# Day 5
# Nurturing Hope in Difficult Times

**Scripture:** "But those who hope in the Lord will renew their strength." **Isaiah 40:31 NIV**

In the quietest hours of the night, when shadows loom large and the road ahead seems lost in the fog, there's a flicker—a small, steady light we know as hope. It's that inner spark that insists, "Keep going," when everything else whispers, "Why bother?" Today, I want to talk about how we can feed that flame, how we can grow that whisper into a voice that roars.

Sometimes life hits hard, testing our faith, and making us question what we believe in. It's in these moments we need to remember all the times hope has seen us through before. It's remembering the sunsets after the storms, the unexpected helping hands, and the moments of strength we never knew we had. Those memories? They're our proof —proof that we've been looked after before, and we will be again.

To keep hope alive, we've got to do our part, too. It means looking for those little signs that things are moving, and changing, even when it's tough. It's about seeking out the good, finding joy in the small things, and believing in the quiet workings of a greater plan. So let's commit to this together: to hold onto hope like a lifeline. By doing so, we're not just wishing on stars—we're navigating by them, steering by God's love, trusting in promises that have stood the test of time. Let's make hope our compass.

**Prayer:** "Lord, nourish my heart with hope, even in the darkest times. Remind me of Your promises and the strength that blooms from steadfast faith. Amen."

**Affirmation:** "My hope is a powerful force that sustains and empowers me."

**Journal Prompt:** Reflect on a hope that has sustained you through a difficult period. How has this hope shaped your journey?

_____

_____

_____

_____

_____

_____

_____

_____

_____

**Challenge:** Write a letter of hope to yourself, detailing the hopes that sustain you and the dreams you wish to pursue, regardless of current challenges.

# Day 6
# The Beauty of Self-Compassion

**Scripture:** "As God's chosen people, holy and dearly loved, clothe yourselves with compassion, kindness, humility, gentleness, and patience." **Colossians 3:12 NIV**

Isn't it a bit strange? We're so quick to offer a shoulder or a kind word to someone else in their tough times, yet we're often our own harshest critics. Let's turn the lens around and shine some of that compassion on ourselves for a change. Self-compassion, it's this beautiful healing practice of giving ourselves a break, of treating ourselves with the gentleness we'd extend to a dear friend.

It's about time we acknowledge that our worth isn't hinged on hitting the mark every single time. We're valued infinitely more than our worst days or missteps. God sees us in a light so loving and forgiving that it can heal all our self-inflicted wounds. By learning to embrace ourselves, quirks and all, we're not only honoring His vision of us but also opening our hearts to a world of grace.

So, as we journey on this path of self-kindness, remember that we're learning to view ourselves through God's eyes, seeing the worthiness that has been there all along. Let's practice self-compassion not just as an act of love for ourselves but as an act of faith, accepting that we too are beloved, valuable, and absolutely deserving of compassion.

**Prayer:** "Heavenly Father, teach me to extend the same compassion to myself that You offer me. In moments of self-doubt, remind me of my worth in Your eyes. Amen."

**Affirmation:** "I treat myself with kindness and compassion."

**Journal Prompt:** Consider areas where you might be too hard on yourself. How can you practice more self-compassion in these areas?

_____

_____

_____

_____

_____

_____

_____

_____

_____

_____

**Challenge:** Treat yourself to a moment of self-care today, doing something that brings you joy and peace, as a practice of self-compassion.

# Day 7
# Reflection and Rest

**Scripture:** "Come to me, all you who are weary and burdened, and I will give you rest." **Matthew 11:28 NIV**

H ere you are, at the close of your very first week , and what a week it's been! It's time to hit the pause button, to take a long, deep breath and just be. Let's take a moment to cozy up in our favorite nook and think about the days that have just passed. Remember those times when you felt exposed, the growing pains of stretching beyond your comfort zone, and the gentle reminders of God's presence cradling us in our most fragile hours.

This pause, this rest, it's not just about giving our bodies a break. It's a sacred time to unload our worries and cares, to let them tumble from our shoulders and into the hands of the One who can carry it all. When we rest, we're not being idle; we're recharging, body and soul, gearing up for the days ahead. It's a quiet rebellion against the hustle of life, affirming that we're more than what we do—we're precious in being.

**Prayer:** "God of Rest, as I reflect on this week, I thank You for the lessons learned and the strength found in vulnerability. Refresh my spirit as I continue this journey."

**Affirmation:** "I give myself permission to rest and reflect."

**Journal Prompt:** Reflect on this week's journey. What insights have you gained about strength in vulnerability?

_____

_____

_____

_____

_____

_____

_____

_____

_____

_____

**Challenge:** Spend some quiet time in nature, reflecting on the week's lessons and the growth you've experienced.

**Interactive Challenge For Week One**
**Week 1: Finding Strength in Vulnerability -**

**Challenge:** Share Your Story

**Description:** Find a quiet moment to share your story with someone you trust. It could be a summary of your week, a particular insight you've gained, or an area where you've felt vulnerable. This act of sharing is a powerful step in embracing vulnerability as strength.

# CHAPTER 02 **WEEK 2**
## HARNESSING INNER RESILIENCE

# Day 8

# Building Mental and Emotional Resilience

**Scripture:** "We are hard pressed on every side, but not crushed; perplexed, but not in despair." **2 Corinthians 4:8 NIV**

R esilience isn't about dodging life's curveballs; it's about suiting up in our spiritual armor and stepping up to bat, no matter how fast the pitches come our way. Think of it as the inner strength that keeps us on our feet when the world seems determined to knock us down. And today, let's work on building up that resilience, just like you'd build muscle: with consistent, dedicated practice.

Consider the trees: they're not rigid, they sway with the winds, but they don't snap. They've got roots that go deep, and that's what we're aiming for—roots that reach into the nourishing soil of faith, that drink up the truth in God's promises. Resilience is learning the art of the bend, the graceful tilt into the wind, knowing we won't break because we're not relying on our own strength; we're leaning on God's.

So today, let's take a conscious step toward that goal. Let's acknowledge that our resilience is a divine gift, honed by our trust in something bigger than ourselves. As we move through the day, let's remind ourselves that our power to persevere isn't measured by how unscathed we are, but by the depth of our faith and the strength that flows from that unshakable bond with the Almighty.

**Prayer:** "Strengthen me, Lord, with the resilience to face any challenge, grounded in Your word and love."

**Affirmation:** "Through challenges, I grow stronger and more resilient."

**Journal Prompt:** Identify a past challenge where you displayed resilience. What helped you persevere?

_____

_____

_____

_____

_____

_____

_____

_____

_____

**Challenge:** Identify a current challenge and one practical step you can take to address it with resilience.

# Day 9
# Overcoming Fear with Faith

**Scripture:** "Fear not, for I am with you; be not dismayed, for I am your God." **Isaiah 41:10 NIV**

Fear can be like an uninvited guest at the table of our minds, filling the conversation with whispers of what-ifs and not-enoughs. Yet, here we are, ready to pull up a chair and meet it eye-to-eye. We've got something fear doesn't expect, a shield named Faith. It's etched with the wisdom that we were never crafted to walk through life handcuffed by fear, but empowered with a spirit of strength, love, and clarity (hello, 2 Timothy 1:7!).

Faith isn't about pretending fear doesn't exist. It's about facing it head-on with an unshakable ally by our side. It's knowing in our bones that we're part of a bigger story, one where every page turn is guided by a hand that writes in the ink of power and love.

Let's dive into the words and promises that have outlasted empires and epochs, letting them light up our path. Let faith be our torch when the path gets dim, our compass when the road twists. Each step we take today, emboldened by faith, is a step out of fear's shadow and into the warm glow of certainty that comes from knowing we're never, ever doing this solo.

**Prayer:** "God of Courage, help me to replace my fears with faith in You. May I rest in the assurance of Your protection and love."

**Affirmation:** "My faith is stronger than my fears."

**Journal Prompt:** How does faith help you confront fears? Can you recall a time when faith diminished your fear?

_____

_____

_____

_____

_____

_____

_____

_____

_____

_____

**Challenge:** Write down your fears and next to each, write a promise from God's word that counters that fear. Pray over these promises.

# Day 10
# Staying Grounded in the Present

**Scripture:** "Therefore do not worry about tomorrow, for tomorrow will worry about itself." **Matthew 6:34 NIV**

Life has a knack for turning into a whirlwind, doesn't it? Before we know it, our minds are sprinting towards tomorrow's to-do list or tripping over yesterdays that can't be changed. But let's hit pause together. Right now, it's about embracing mindfulness, about finding that quiet center in the midst of the chaos—the sweet spot where we can hear God's whisper.

Think of Mary, right there in the clutter of daily life, choosing the better part: to be present, to listen, to be still at the feet of Jesus. There's wisdom there for us, too. It's in the art of being fully here, in this moment, that we find true peace. It's where we can see the blessings tucked in our day, the lessons that only "now" can teach us.

So let's make a promise to ourselves: to trust God with our tomorrows, to find our joy not in the what-ifs and the should-haves, but right here in the living, breathing now. It's in the present that we find God, ourselves, and the simple beauty of being.

**Prayer:** "Lord, teach me to live in the present, where Your grace is sufficient, and Your presence is a constant comfort."

**Affirmation:** "I live in the present, embracing each moment with peace and clarity."

**Journal Prompt:** What practices help you stay present? How does being present affect your resilience?

_____

_____

_____

_____

_____

_____

_____

_____

_____

**Challenge:** Practice mindfulness or meditation today, focusing on the present moment and God's presence in it.

# Day 11
# The Strength in Letting Go

**Scripture:** "Cast all your anxiety on him because he cares for you."
**1 Peter 5:7 NIV**

It's funny how we clench our fists around the reins of life, thinking if we just hold on tight enough, we can steer clear of the unknown. Here's a little secret: there's incredible power in uncurling those fingers, in letting go. Today, let's talk about that—about surrendering not to defeat, but to the freedom and strength that come from trust.

Imagine you're holding a balloon, your worries scribbled on its surface. Now picture releasing it into the sky, watching it drift away. That's what we're doing when we surrender our troubles to something higher—God's loving hands. It's not giving up; it's giving over, believing that He can take what we let go of and shape it with His love and wisdom.

When we do this, there's a surprising gift that comes along for the ride: peace. It's the peace that seeps in when we acknowledge that our concerns are now being carried by the One who has always been walking with us, leading us toward outcomes that are beyond our best planning. Let's lean into that peace today, together.

**Prayer:** "Heavenly Father, grant me the wisdom to let go of what I cannot change."

**Affirmation:** "I find strength and peace in letting go of what I cannot control."

**Journal Prompt:** Reflect on something you're holding onto that's not serving you. How might letting it go improve your resilience?

_____

_____

_____

_____

_____

_____

_____

_____

_____

_____

**Challenge:** Choose one thing you've struggled to let go of and commit to a small action today that symbolizes releasing it to God.

# Day 12
# Perseverance Through Adversity

**Scripture:** "But those who hope in the Lord will renew their strength." **Isaiah 40:31 NIV**

Walking the path of faith isn't always a stroll through sunny meadows; sometimes it's a climb up steep and rocky paths. On days like these, we can take a leaf out of the lives of folks like Job and Paul. Imagine them, not as distant, saintly figures, but as people who stubbed their toes on the boulders of life, just like we do. They faced the storms head-on and stayed rooted in their faith, not because they had no doubts or pain, but because they knew where their strength came from.

Perseverance is more than just gritting your teeth and bearing it; it's about blossoming through the cracks of hardship. It's when we lean not on our own understanding but on the solid ground of God's grace. Today, let's look at our challenges as more than just obstacles to get past. They're opportunities—rich soil where our spiritual roots can dig deep, drawing nourishment from every lesson learned.

Let's take a moment today to see our trials differently: not dead as ends, but as fertile soil. Within each difficulty lies a seed that can bloom into a more hopeful, trust-filled version of us. Let's nurture these seeds with God's redeeming love and watch as we, too, blossom into endurance with a purpose.

**Prayer:** "Lord of Perseverance, in moments of adversity, remind me of Your enduring love and the strength I possess through You to overcome."

**Affirmation:** "I am filled with enduring strength and hope."

**Journal Prompt:** Think of a time you wanted to give up but didn't. What motivated you to keep going?

_____

_____

_____

_____

_____

_____

_____

_____

_____

_____

**Challenge:** Identify a current adversity. Set a small, achievable goal that represents perseverance and commit to it today.

# Day 13
# Learning from Life's Challenges

**Scripture:** "Consider it pure joy, my brothers and sisters, whenever you face trials of many kinds." – **James 1:2 NIV**

Y ou know, the road of faith isn't just lined with cheering crowds and victory laps; it often loops through valleys of shadow, with hills that test our inner strength at every turn. I've felt it, you've probably felt it—we're in good company, really. Take Job or Paul from the good old Bible tales; they faced the kind of challenges that would make anyone's knees buckle, yet they clung to their faith like a lifeline.

Here's the heart of it: perseverance isn't just surviving; it's allowing ourselves to be transformed by the trials we endure. It's about discovering a fortitude we didn't know we had, which comes from a source far greater than our own. When we lean on God's unwavering strength and grace, we're not just getting by, we're growing—blossoming under pressure, turning hardships into lessons, and lessons into stepping stones.

Pause; look at your struggles through a different lens. View them as rich soil for our growth, as the tough stuff that can make us more resilient, more compassionate, and more grounded in hope. With every challenge, let's remind ourselves that we're not just pushing through—we're being shaped, molded, and loved into stronger, wiser souls, sculpted by God's own hand.

**Prayer:** "Teacher of All, help me to see the lessons in every challenge and to grow in wisdom and character through them."

**Affirmation:** "Every challenge is an opportunity for growth and learning."

**Journal Prompt:** What is a significant lesson you've learned from a past challenge? How has it shaped who you are today?

_____

_____

_____

_____

_____

_____

_____

_____

_____

_____

**Challenge:** Share the lesson you've reflected on today with someone close to you, discussing how it has influenced your growth.

# Day 14
# Learning from Life's Challenges

**Scripture:** "Give thanks in all circumstances; for this is God's will for you in Christ Jesus." – **1 Thessalonians 5:18 NIV**

We've turned another page on our calendar, and here we are wrapping up the second week of this soul-nourishing journey together. Let's hit the brakes for a day, breathe in deeply, and bask in the rearview mirror of the past seven days. Even when the road got bumpy, there were moments—little sparks—where we could see God's hand at work, could feel His presence, quiet but potent, in every step we took.

Turning our gaze towards gratitude isn't just about being thankful; it's a shift in perspective, a lens that colors what we see. It's moving our eyes from the empty spaces to the fullness of our lives, the small victories, the whispers of progress, the unexpected joys that have a way of showing up right when we need them.

Take a moment to celebrate the resilience that's budding inside you, the wisdom you've gathered, and the quiet, steadfast grace that's been our constant companion. Here's to the lessons, the blessings, and everything in between.

**Prayer:** "God of Gratitude, as I reflect on this week, I thank You for the strength You've nurtured in me and for the blessings, both seen and unseen."

**Affirmation:** "I choose gratitude, finding reasons to be thankful each day."

**Journal Prompt:** Reflect on the past week. What moments of resilience stand out to you, and for what are you most grateful?

_____

_____

_____

_____

_____

_____

_____

_____

_____

_____

**Challenge:** Write down three things from the past week you are grateful for, especially related to resilience. Share one of these with a friend or family member, expressing your gratitude.

## Interactive Challenge For Week Two

**Week 2: Harnessing Inner Resilience - Challenge**

**Challenge:** Resilience Reflection

**Description:** Reflect on a recent challenge and how you responded to it. Write down or discuss with a friend what resilience meant in this situation. Identify one area where you showed strength and one where you wish to grow.

# CHAPTER 03  WEEK 3
## CULTIVATING PEACE & HEALING

# Day 15
# Finding Peace Amidst the Storm

**Scripture:** "Peace I leave with you; my peace I give you. I do not give to you as the world gives. Do not let your hearts be troubled and do not be afraid." – **John 14:27 NIV**

Amid the whirlwind of daily chaos, where peace feels like a distant dream, there's an open invitation from God to step into the quiet center he holds just for us. It's this sweet spot, the eye of the storm, where stillness lives and the world's turmoil can't touch us. Let's dive into that today, into the extraordinary kind of peace that doesn't even make sense sometimes—peace that's not about everything being perfect, but about feeling grounded even when it's all spinning around us.

This peace, the kind Jesus talks about, it's not like anything we find elsewhere. It's not a temporary patch or a fragile truce. It's solid, generous, and waiting for us whenever we decide to reach for it. As we're tossed by life's waves, let's plant our feet firmly in the love that doesn't shift with the tides, the love that promises we're never adrift when we make our home in God's heart.

So, as we move through today's highs and lows, let's remind ourselves that peace isn't an elusive butterfly to catch—it's a constant presence, there for us the moment we choose to lean into it, to settle down into the safety of God's arms. True peace? It's ours for the taking, always there in His unwavering embrace.

**Prayer:** "Lord of Peace, in the midst of life's storms, be my calm. Help me to find Your peace that surpasses all understanding."

**Affirmation:** "In the midst of turmoil, I find a deep and lasting peace within me."

**Journal Prompt:** Reflect on a tumultuous time in your life. How did you find peace amidst the chaos?

_____

_____

_____

_____

_____

_____

_____

_____

_____

_____

**Challenge:** Identify a current source of stress or chaos in your life. Dedicate 15 minutes to pray, specifically seeking God's peace in this situation.

# Day 16
# The Healing Power of Nature

**Scripture:** The Lord is my shepherd, I lack nothing. He makes me lie down in green pastures; he leads me beside quiet waters." – **Psalms 23:1-2 NIV**

Chemotherapy made me sensitive to the sun, a challenge since I found comfort in its rays. Determined not to lose this part of my routine, I adapted. I placed a chair on the shaded side of my house, removed my shoes, and pressed my feet into the grass. It was a simple act, but sitting there brought me a profound sense of peace.

This spot became my refuge, a place to relax and recharge. Nature's presence—its beauty and stillness—offered a reminder of life's bigger picture. The elements, from the wind to the songs of birds, seemed to embody a calmness that was both grounding and healing.

God's creation is a testament to His majesty and care, a source of healing and peace for weary souls. Today, we're reminded of the rejuvenating power found in the beauty of nature—the whisper of the wind, the chorus of birds, the steadfastness of mountains. These elements of creation reflect the Creator's own peace and stability. As we step into the natural world, let's allow our senses to be filled with the wonder of God's handiwork, finding in it a healing balm for both body and spirit.

**Prayer:** "Creator God, thank You for the healing beauty of Your creation. Help me to see Your hand in the simplicity and serenity of nature."

**Affirmation:** "Nature's beauty and tranquility are healing balm to my soul."

**Journal Prompt: Think of a moment when you felt a deep connection to nature and experienced its healing effect. What was special about that time?**

_____
_____
_____
_____
_____
_____
_____
_____
_____
_____

**Challenge:** Spend time outdoors today, whether it's a walk in the park, sitting by a body of water, or simply standing under a tree. Reflect on the sense of peace and healing it brings.

# Day 17
# Meditation and Mindfulness

**Scripture:** "Be still, and know that I am God." – **Psalms 46:10 NIV**

In the whirlwind of daily life, it's easy to forget to pause. But there's a whisper amidst the chaos, a gentle reminder: 'Be still and know that I am God.' It's an invitation, not just to slow down, but to delve into the quiet depths of meditation and mindfulness. These aren't just practices; they're pathways to peace—the kind of peace that settles deep in your soul.

So, let's take a breath. Close your eyes. Let the world fade just a bit as you focus on the here and now, on God's word, on His reassuring presence. It's in this space that we anchor ourselves against life's storms.

Make it a habit, carve out a moment in your day to just be. To listen—not for the loud and the urgent, but for the soft and the significant. It's in these moments that we're truly present, that we live the fullness of the moments given to us. Let's step into this practice together, finding stillness in a bustling world and clarity in our hearts through the presence of God. Remember, it's not about carving out hours from your day; it's about the quality of the moments you dedicate to being truly present.

**Prayer:** "God of the Present Moment, teach me the art of mindfulness, to live fully in each moment, experiencing Your presence in all things."

**Affirmation:** "In stillness and mindfulness, I connect deeply with my inner peace."

**Journal Prompt:** How does being mindful or meditative affect your day-to-day life? Can you recall a specific instance where mindfulness brought you clarity or peace?

_____

_____

_____

_____

_____

_____

_____

_____

_____

_____

**Challenge:** Practice a mindfulness exercise today. This could be meditating on scripture, mindful eating, or simply observing your breath for a few minutes without distraction.

# Day 18
# The Art of Patience in Healing

**Scripture:** "But if we hope for what we do not see, we wait for it with patience." – **Romans 8:25 NIV**

Sometimes, it feels like healing is a long road—one that meanders at its own pace, much to our frustration. I've come to see this process, whether it's mending a broken bone or a broken heart, as something that can't be rushed. It unfolds, bit by bit, in a rhythm set by something greater than us. This is where patience becomes not just a virtue, but a companion on the journey.

Imagine a tiny seed. In the quiet earth, it lies in wait, embraced by darkness. It's not idle though; it's preparing. It's a period full of potential, of energy that's gathering for the right moment to burst forth into life. We're like that seed during our times of healing. There may be moments when we feel buried by our circumstances, clouded by uncertainty, but underneath, growth is stirring.

Honor your personal seasons of growth. Embrace the wait, the stillness, the slow unfolding of progress. Every second of anticipation is wrapped in a purpose, and in the grand tapestry of life, every thread of patience is a stroke of the Creator's design. Know that you are cradled in caring hands, and that the waiting itself is part of a larger plan, a narrative of healing authored by divine timing. Take this to heart, and remember that patience is not just waiting; it's growing in the wait.

**Prayer:** "Patient Father, in times of waiting, fortify my spirit with Your patience, trusting in Your timing for my healing and growth."

**Affirmation:** "With patience, I embrace my healing journey, trusting in the process."

**Journal Prompt:** Reflect on a time when being patient was challenging but ultimately led to healing or growth.

---------------------------------------------------------------
---------------------------------------------------------------
---------------------------------------------------------------
---------------------------------------------------------------
---------------------------------------------------------------
---------------------------------------------------------------
---------------------------------------------------------------
---------------------------------------------------------------
---------------------------------------------------------------
---------------------------------------------------------------

**Challenge:** Identify one area of your life where you're seeking change or healing. Commit to practicing patience in this area, reminding yourself of God's timing.

# Day 19
# Embracing Change and Growth

**Scripture:** "See, I am doing a new thing! Now it springs up; do you not perceive it?" – **Isaiah 43:19 NIV**

Change—inevitable and constant, like the ebb and flow of the tide. It can be unsettling, sure, but it's also ripe with promise for personal transformation. Today, let's shift our perspective to see change not as a hurdle, but as an open invitation to deepen our faith and our connection to something greater.

Life's twists and turns are not just mere happenstance; they are part of a divine dance, guiding us toward becoming our truest selves. A new beginning, the raw ache of loss, or even the leap of faith into uncharted territory—each is a chance to stretch our spiritual muscles, to grow in ways we never imagined.

As we navigate these changes, let's hold onto the belief that we're not adrift in this journey. We have a compass that points us toward renewal and growth. Trust that in every shift, every new direction, there's a purpose. God's presence is the constant in every change, the steady hand on our shoulder steering us forward, molding our hearts with each step. Let's walk confidently into the unknown, buoyed by the faith that every change is a step towards becoming more aligned with the divine blueprint for our lives. Keep this mindset close to heart: each change is a stepping stone on your path, not just to where you're going, but to who you're becoming.

**Prayer:** "God of transformation, as I face changes and challenges, help me to embrace them as opportunities for growth, trusting that You are molding me for the better."

**Affirmation:** "I embrace change, seeing it as a pathway to growth and new beginnings."

**Journal Prompt:** Consider a change you've recently faced. How did it contribute to your personal growth?

_____

_____

_____

_____

_____

_____

_____

_____

_____

**Challenge:** Identify one change you're currently resisting. Take a small step today to accept and embrace this change, focusing on the potential growth it offers.

# Day 20
# The Comfort of Routine and Ritual

**Scripture:** "Your word is a lamp for my feet, a light on my path." – **Psalms 119:105 NIV**

In the midst of life's constant twists and turns, there's a profound solace to be found in our daily rituals. These moments of calm—the morning prayer whispered before the day begins, the verses of scripture that fill the quiet corners of the evening, the melodies of worship that echo through the walls of our hearts—act as anchors, steadying us amidst the storm of change.

As we go about our day today, let's take a moment to appreciate these personal practices. They're more than habits; they're sacred appointments with the divine, moments where we can meet with God and tune in to the quiet stirrings of our souls. It's in these consistent acts of devotion that we find a sense of peace that transcends understanding.

These rituals do much more than ground us; they pull us closer to the heart of God. They are a testament to His unwavering presence, a daily reminder that, no matter the chaos around us, His grace moves with a rhythm that is constant and true.

Embrace your rituals. Let them be calm in your chaos, the space where you connect with someone greater than yourself, and the reminder of his unchanging faithfulness.

**Prayer:** "God of order, bless my daily routines and rituals. Let them be a source of comfort and peace, anchoring me in Your grace."

**Affirmation:** "In my routines and rituals, I find comfort and guidance."

**Journal Prompt:** What daily routine or ritual brings you comfort and a sense of peace? Why do you think it has this effect?

_____

_____

_____

_____

_____

_____

_____

_____

_____

_____

**Challenge:** If you don't already have a daily routine or ritual that brings you peace, create one today. It could be as simple as morning prayer, a short walk, or a bedtime gratitude practice. Commit to it for the next week.

# Day 21
# Reflecting on Progress

**Scripture:** "I thank my God every time I remember you."
**– Philippians 1:3 NIV**

As we wrap up this third week, it's time to press pause and turn inward, taking stock of our journey toward peace and healing. This act of reflection isn't just about patting ourselves on the back for the miles walked. It's about realizing that we haven't been walking alone. With every step, every stumble, every stride forward, there's been a guiding presence. So let's take a deep breath and offer gratitude—not only for the calm that's slowly been woven into our days or the beginnings of healing weaving through our hearts but for the unseen hand that's been holding ours along the way.

Celebrate the progress, the patience, and the grace that's brought you here. Remember that healing is a path, not a destination, and every step on that path is part of an extraordinary process.

**Prayer:** "God of Growth, thank You for the progress I've made and the journey I'm on. Help me to continue growing in peace and healing, ever closer to You."

**Affirmation:** "I celebrate my progress and the journey that has shaped me."

**Journal Prompt:** Look back over the past three weeks. What progress have you made in finding peace and cultivating healing in your life?

_____

_____

_____

_____

_____

_____

_____

_____

_____

_____

**Challenge:** Write down three ways you've grown in the last three weeks. Share this progress with a friend, family member, or in your journal, and set one goal for continuing this growth in the coming weeks.

## Interactive Challenge For Week Three
### Week 3: Cultivating Peace and Healing - Challenge

**Challenge:** Create a Peace Ritual

**Description:** Design a simple ritual or activity that brings you peace. It could be a short walk, a tea ceremony, a few minutes of deep breathing, or a particular prayer. Practice this daily, observing how it influences your sense of peace and healing.

# CHAPTER 04  WEEK 4
## EMBRACING A NEW PERSPECTIVE

# Day 22
# Finding Joy in Small Moments

**Scripture:** "This is the day the Lord has made; we will rejoice and be glad in it." – **Psalms 118:24 NIV**

Have you ever noticed how the simplest things can bring the greatest happiness? That burst of laughter when you're with friends, the way the sky paints itself in brilliant colors as the sun dips below the horizon, or the quiet comfort that comes from a verse you've known by heart since childhood. Today, make it your mission to seek out these tiny, perfect moments of joy.

They're more than just happy accidents; they're little presents, wrapped up in the ordinary, waiting to be discovered. Each time we stumble upon one of these treasures, it's like a gentle reminder from the divine to stay awake to the wonder all around us. With each moment we gather, our days begin to change, taking on a richer hue.

Start nurturing a habit of joy-hunting. With every sunrise, anticipate the laughter, the beauty, and the comfort that await us. As we collect these moments, let's allow them to buoy our spirits, weaving us ever closer into the joyful heart of God.

**Prayer:** "God of Joy, open my eyes to the small moments of joy around me. Help me to cherish and seek them daily."

**Affirmation:** "I find joy in every day and in the small moments that make life beautiful."

**Journal Prompt:** Identify a small joy you experienced today. Why was it significant?

_____

_____

_____

_____

_____

_____

_____

_____

_____

_____

**Challenge:** Identify a current adversity. Set a small, achievable goal that represents perseverance and commit to it today.

# Day 23
# The Value of Deep Connections

**Scripture:** "A friend loves at all times, and a brother is born for a time of adversity." – **Proverbs 17:17 NIV**

In this winding road of life, it's the people we share our journey with that add color to our days—our family, who've known us since day one, our friends who become our chosen family, and our faith communities that support our spiritual walk. Today, let's make it a priority to really see the value in these relationships. They are the gardens where love blooms most vividly, the places where God's love comes to life in a smile, a hug, or a listening ear.

When we dare to deepen these bonds, we're not just opening ourselves to others; we're building a sanctuary of shared strength, support, and belonging. There's an incredible power in that—to know and to be known, to love and be loved. This is where we find the courage to be our most authentic selves, and the comfort that no matter what, we're not alone.

Put your heart into cultivating these relationships, cherishing them as precious channels through which grace and love flow. As you do, you grow, not just in your capacity to receive love, but in your ability to give it. In each act of kindness, each moment of connection, we reflect and multiply the empathy and love that knit us together.

**Prayer:** "Father of Connection, thank You for the deep relationships in my life. Help me to nurture these bonds with Your love and grace."

**Affirmation:** "I cherish the deep connections in my life, recognizing their value and strength."

**Journal Prompt:** Reflect on a relationship that has deepened recently. What have you learned from this connection?

_____

_____

_____

_____

_____

_____

_____

_____

_____

_____

**Challenge:** Reach out to someone with whom you have a deep connection. Share your appreciation for their presence in your life.

# Day 24
# Cultivating a Grateful Heart

**Scripture:** "Let the peace of Christ rule in your hearts... And be thankful." – **Colossians 3:15 NIV**

Embracing gratitude can transform the way we see our world and ourselves. It's like flipping a switch that turns on the light of positivity, illuminating the goodness that's often overshadowed by our wants and worries. Today, let's lean into this transformative practice.

You know, gratitude isn't just about saying 'thank you' for the big things; it's also about noticing the little kindnesses, the quiet blessings, the moments and people that make our lives richer just by being part of them. Each one is a note in the symphony of goodness that plays around us—a symphony orchestrated by a higher power.

Let's not save gratitude for special occasions. Make it as natural as breathing—part of your everyday routine. As you acknowledge the good, you're not just enriching your own spirit; you're also giving a nod to the universe, to the divine force that sustains and nourishes us all.

Cultivate this habit, and watch as it reshapes your perspective, strengthens your faith, and throws into sharp relief the myriad ways love is woven into your life. By living gratefully, you become an active participant in a world brimming with grace.

**Prayer:** "Gracious God, cultivate in me a heart of gratitude. Let me always be quick to see Your blessings and express my thanks."

**Affirmation:** "I cultivate a heart full of gratitude, which transforms my perspective and brings peace."

**Journal Prompt:** What are three things you're grateful for today? How does gratitude shape your perspective?

_____

_____

_____

_____

_____

_____

_____

_____

_____

_____

**Challenge:** Start each day this week by listing three things you're grateful for. Notice how this practice influences your day.

# Day 25
# Learning New Ways to Love Life

**Scripture:** "I have come that they may have life, and have it to the full." – **John 10:10 NIV**

The world's a playground. You've heard it before, right? Well, sometimes, we forget that we're still allowed to play. The beauty of this life, this incredible, diverse creation of God's, is that it's brimming with hidden nooks and crannies waiting to be discovered by us. It's a personal invitation to not just exist, but to thrive, to color outside the lines, to learn a new dance step in the rhythm of life.

Today, I'm here to nudge you—yes, you—to light that spark of curiosity that's been waiting for a bit of oxygen. Grab a paintbrush, lace up your hiking boots, volunteer, or lose yourself in a book. Every new hobby or interest is a thread, and when we weave these threads together, they add a richness to our tapestry that was never there before.

It's in these moments, when we're elbow-deep in paint or soil, when we're lost in service or study, that we might just hear God's whispers over our shoulder, feel His presence in our laughter and concentration. Jump into the adventure of your own life, wholeheartedly, with the trust that in our joy and exploration, we're delighting the heart of God. What is the purpose of living if you don't have a life?

**Prayer:** "Inventive Creator, inspire me to discover new passions and joys. In them, let me find new ways to love the life You've given me."

**Affirmation:** "I embrace life fully, constantly learning and finding new passions that bring joy."

**Journal Prompt:** Explore a new hobby or interest that could bring joy into your life. What draws you to it?

_____

_____

_____

_____

_____

_____

_____

_____

_____

_____

**Challenge:** Dedicate time this week to try a new hobby or activity. Reflect on the experience and how it brought joy to your day.

# Day 26
# The Journey of Self-Discovery

**Scripture:** "For we are God's masterpiece. He has created us anew in Christ Jesus, so we can do the good things he planned for us long ago." – **Ephesians 2:10 NLT**

L et's talk about a journey that's not measured in miles but in moments of clarity—the kind that reshapes everything. It's about peering into the mirror of our souls with a little help from above. You see, getting to know the person staring back at us is a vital piece of the puzzle on this spiritual hike we're on.

Today's about digging deep. We're going to sift through our thoughts and feelings, unearth our talents (because we've all got them), and get cozy with our purpose—the one sketched out by God's divine hand. This kind of soul-searching? It's how we strike gold, finding nuggets of truth about who we are and the masterpiece we're meant to be. Every little revelation about our quirks and qualities is a note from God, reminding us of His craftsmanship.

So, embrace today with an open heart, ready to celebrate the one-of-a-kind creation you are. Determined to let our lives sing praises not just with our lips but with every action, every choice, every breath. Here's to the reflections of His glory we're meant to be—imperfect, yes, but oh so wonderfully, super awesomely (Yes, I made up a word.) and perfectly made.

**Prayer:** "God of Discovery, on this journey of self-discovery, help me to understand myself better and to grow in Your light."

**Affirmation:** "I am on a journey of self-discovery, uncovering the masterpiece that I am."

**Journal Prompt:** Reflect on a recent discovery you've made about yourself. How has this insight contributed to your personal growth?

_____

_____

_____

_____

_____

_____

_____

_____

_____

_____

**Challenge:** Share this new insight about yourself with someone close to you, discussing how it has impacted your view of yourself and your life.

# Day 27
# Embracing a Future of Possibilities

**Scripture:** "For I know the plans I have for you," declares the Lord, "plans to prosper you and not to harm you, plans to give you hope and a future." – **Jeremiah 29:11 NIV**

Life's canvas is sprawling, splashed with infinite colors, and every day is an opportunity to pick up a brush and add our own stroke. Let's take today to try something that makes our soul sing, something new that sparks a light in our eyes. It could be picking up a paintbrush, planting a garden, lending a hand where it's needed, or soaking up words that stir the mind.

Diving into a fresh passion or curiosity isn't just about having fun; it's about listening to the pulse of life, feeling it beckon us into a dance of discovery. These new ventures can be paths where joy bubbles up, where God's voice might just surprise us in the rustling of leaves or the swirl of a paintbrush.

So, what do you say? Let's chase the thrill of the new, the buzz of exploration. Who knows what doors it'll swing open? Let's trust in the adventure, with the knowledge that our joy is God's joy, our wonder, His delight.

**Prayer:** "Lord of Possibilities, fill my heart with hope for the future. Guide me towards a life filled with Your promise and potential."

**Affirmation:** "I look forward to a future filled with hope and endless possibilities."

**Journal Prompt:** Envision your future filled with possibilities. What hopes and dreams do you have?

_____

_____

_____

_____

_____

_____

_____

_____

_____

_____

**Challenge:** Create a vision board that represents your hopes and dreams for the future. Place it somewhere you can see daily.

# Day 28
# Celebrating the Steps Taken

**Scripture:** "Give thanks to the Lord, for he is good; his love endures forever." – **Psalms 107:1 NIV**

I magine you're standing at the base of a towering mountain, its peak lost in the clouds. That's the feeling I felt when my cancer diagnosis weighed on my shoulders. I felt overwhelmed looking at the journey ahead. The end was nowhere in sight and I couldn't see the path. At that moment I remembered the African proverb How do you eat an elephant? "It's one bite at a time," I said out loud.

Today, as we round off our 30-day journey. We're celebrating, not just the distance we've traveled but how we've grown and flourished along the way. You've faced your own mountains, you've learned the power of one bite at a time, the courage of persistence, and the strength that comes from a well of faith that runs deep.

This isn't just a pause to catch our breath; it's a moment to cast a grateful eye over the path we've tread. It's been rough in spots, sure, but look at the view from here, the challenges turned to victories, the hard-won wisdom. Today's celebration is a tip of the hat to every hurdle crossed, to God's ever-present guidance, to the companionship we've found in each other. As we look to the horizon, ready for the next leg of the journey, let's carry forward with faith in our steps and love as our compass.

**Prayer:** "God of Celebration, thank You for every step of progress and for the journey we've shared. Bless my continued path with Your presence."

**Affirmation:** "I celebrate every step of my journey, thankful for the love and growth each day brings."

**Journal Prompt:** Celebrate the progress you've made over this devotional. What are the most significant steps you've taken?

_____
_____
_____
_____
_____
_____
_____
_____
_____
_____

**Challenge:** Plan a small celebration of your journey. It could be a quiet moment of reflection, a special meal, or sharing your experiences with others.

## Interactive Challenge for Week Four
### Week 4: Embracing a New Perspective - Challenge

**Challenge:** Joy Journaling

**Description:** For one week, keep a 'Joy Journal.' Each day, write down three things that brought you joy, no matter how small. At the end of the week, review your journal and reflect on the new perspectives and joys you've discovered.

**Final Two Days:** Looking Forward - Challenge

# CHAPTER 05  WEEK 5
# THE FINAL COUNTDOWN

# The Final Countdown

Week by week, we've been trekking together, haven't we? Each step has taken us through the lush valleys and over the rocky ridges of our spiritual lives. We've embraced our raw edges, those vulnerable parts of us that we often hide away. We've built up our resilience like a spiritual muscle, learning to sway with life's storms rather than break against them. We've sought and found pockets of peace in the day's hustle and turned our gaze to view our world through the warm filters of gratitude and hope.

Now, as we come to a gentle stop, it's not the end. It's more like a quiet rest stop on this beautiful path we're walking with God. Let's take every lesson, every shard of light and wisdom we've gathered, and pack it up for the road ahead. Our journey is far from over; in fact, it's an ongoing adventure, one that calls us to keep moving, keep seeking, and keep growing closer to God with each new dawn.

So, as we wrap up this chapter, remember that the insights we've gained are like provisions for the soul—meant to sustain us, to nourish us on the way forward. Let's step out again, with the sun on our faces and the wind at our backs, walking ever closer to God, our ultimate guide.

# Day 29
# Envisioning a Brighter Tomorrow

**Scripture:** "The path of the righteous is like the morning sun, shining ever brighter till the full light of day." – **Proverbs 4:18 ESV**

We're just a heartbeat away from wrapping up this spiritual trek we embarked on together. Today is about painting our tomorrows not with the usual palette of worries but with the vibrant hues of God's love and the sparkling light of His grace. Imagine standing at the brink of a horizon ablaze with possibilities, a future where every hope is a seed planted by divine hands.

This isn't about scribbling down resolutions or sketching out blueprints for the days to come. It's so much more. It's about tuning our dreams to the frequency of God's intentions, marching to the beat of His benevolent plan for us. He's the artist who started this good work within us, and He'll be the one to dot the last i and cross the final t.

So let's devote today to daydreaming with the Almighty. Let's ask Him to weave His wishes into the fabric of our desires, to lead us down paths that bloom with His glory. As we look toward tomorrow, let's do it hand in hand with God, anticipating the "masterpeace" He's ready to unveil through us.

**Prayer:** "Lord of Tomorrow, as I look to the future, fill my heart with dreams and my path with Your light. Guide me toward a future that reflects Your love and fulfills Your purpose for me."

**Affirmation:** "Each day brings me closer to a brighter future, filled with light and hope."

**Journal Prompt:** Imagine yourself one year from now, having fully embraced the lessons from this devotional. What changes do you see in your life?

_____

_____

_____

_____

_____

_____

_____

_____

_____

**Challenge:** Write a letter to your future self, detailing your hopes, dreams, and the spiritual lessons you wish to carry forward. Seal it and set a reminder to open it one year from now.

# Day 30
# A Commitment to Ongoing Growth & Hope

**Scripture:** "Being confident of this, that he who began a good work in you will carry it on to completion until the day of Christ Jesus."
**– Philippians 1:6 NIV**

**H**ere we are, at the final waypost of our current journey together. It's like reaching the end of a trail on a mountain hike, where we've navigated both the climbs and the descents. Take a look at the view from this vantage point, look back to appreciate the terrain we've covered, all the while gearing up for the continued adventure ahead.

We're not just marking a waypoint; we're charting a course forward, reaffirming our commitment to pursue a life that mirrors Christ more with each passing day. Keep trekking with purpose. Know that everyday will not be easy but His Grace is Sufficient. Continue this expedition of faith, letting every lesson learned, every ounce of strength gathered, and every burst of joy experienced equip us for the journey to come. This is our moment of promise.

**Prayer:** "Eternal God, as this devotional journey concludes, my commitment to You and my growth in faith does not. Empower me to continue seeking You, growing in Your grace, and living out the truths I've embraced. You said your grace is sufficient so I ask you for Grace, Grace, a double portion of your Grace to help me continue this journey with Unshakable Faith."

**Affirmation:** "I am committed to my journey of growth and hope, trusting in the beautiful process of becoming."

**Journal Prompt:** Reflect on the commitment you're willing to make for your ongoing spiritual growth. How will you continue to nurture the seeds planted during this devotional?

_____

_____

_____

_____

_____

_____

_____

_____

_____

_____

**Challenge:** Create a spiritual growth plan for the next year. Include regular practices such as prayer, meditation, scripture reading, and any other activities that have enriched your journey. Schedule monthly check-ins with yourself to assess your progress and adjust as needed.

# CHAPTER 06  WEEK 6
## EMBRACING AN UNSHAKEABLE SPIRIT

# Reflections on the Journey

As we stand on the threshold of the final day of our 30-day journey, we pause to look back at the path we've traversed together. From the initial steps of acknowledging our vulnerability and finding strength in it, to harnessing inner resilience, cultivating peace and healing, and finally, embracing joy and a hopeful future — each day has been a step towards a deeper understanding of our unshakable spirit in the face of life's storms.

This journey was not just about facing the challenges of cancer or the trials of life; it was about discovering the immense power of faith, hope, and love that resides within us all. It was about learning to lean on God's strength in our weakest moments and finding peace in His presence amidst turmoil.

## Growth and Transformation

Reflect on the moments of growth and transformation you've experienced throughout these 30 days. Each scripture read, every prayer whispered, and all reflections pondered have been bricks in the foundation of your renewed spirit. You've learned to see vulnerability as a strength, to embrace change as an opportunity for growth, and to find joy in the simplest moments.

Your journal pages are a testament to your journey, filled with honest reflections, heartfelt prayers, and aspirations for the future. These pages hold the essence of your transformation — a transformation that has prepared you to face the future with an unshakable faith.

## Looking Forward

As we close this chapter, remember that the end of this devotional does not signify the end of your journey. Your path of growth, discovery, and healing continues beyond these pages. Carry forward the lessons learned, the strength gained, and the peace found as you move forward.

Commit to keeping your faith as your guiding light, allowing it to illuminate the path ahead. Continue to seek moments of connection with God through prayer, reflection, and gratitude. Let the unshakable spirit you've nurtured be your compass, leading you towards a future filled with hope, love, and the infinite possibilities that await when you place your trust in the Lord.

# Final Prayer

"Heavenly Father, as we conclude this devotional journey, we thank You for being our unwavering source of strength, comfort, and hope. We stand in awe of the work You have done in our hearts and lives through these thirty days. Guide us as we continue on our path, keeping our spirits rooted in Your love and our faith unshakable in the face of life's storms. Amen."

# Final Affirmation

"I AM A MASTERPEACE. My faith is strong, my spirit is resilient, and my heart is filled with hope. I move forward with God as my guide, ready to face whatever comes my way with courage, grace, and a joyful heart."

www.ingramcontent.com/pod-product-compliance
Lightning Source LLC
Chambersburg PA
CBHW031230120626
46545CB00003B/1070